Got Anger?

Eliane Herdani, PhD

Creative and Therapeutic Solutions to Everyday Anger Issues

Limits of Liability and Disclaimer of Warranty

The author and publisher shall not be liable for your misuse of this material. This book is strictly for informational and educational purposes.

Warning – Disclaimer

The purpose of this book is to educate and entertain. The author and/or publisher do not guarantee that anyone following these techniques, suggestions, tips, ideas, or strategies will become successful. The author and/or publisher shall have neither liability nor responsibility to anyone with respect to any loss or damage caused, or alleged to be caused, directly or indirectly, by the information contained in this book.

DEDICATION

Dedicated to all my clients and people that work hard in changing unhealthy anger into constructive and transformatory anger.

CONTENTS

Eliane Herdani, PhD

ACKNOWLEDGMENTS

There are many people that have shown me the way on my journey. My parents who laid a safe and open-minded foundation; my aunt who always showed enthusiasm for my endeavors and my friends who support me and cheer me up during hard times. I am grateful to all of them.

In addition, I am very thankful to my husband who is always ready to give kind and loving words of encouragement, my beautiful daughters who teach me every day and keep me on track and finally to Donna Kozik for her knowledge, and good-humored self. Lori Miller for her efficiency and Jamie Gifford for the thorough and detailed edits on the text. Last, but not least, Bobbi Linkemer, to assist on the final birthing process.

Dear Reader,

my work as a psychotherapist allows me to take a peek into people's lives and minds. Clients come with diverse issues plaguing them, and in many cases, anger seems to be a part of the problem, whether it is suppressed, expressed or denied. As humankind we are doing much better, in comparison to the extreme anger aggression done by our ancestors, yet we still have improvements to make on how to "do anger" in a constructive way.

This book is a contribution to the good anger movement. It provides creative and therapeutic strategies on how to deal with and heal from destructive anger.

I hope this book can be the start of a new healing journey for you, and I would love to connect with you through my website www.lifeaspects.com.

With all my love,

Eliane

CHAPTER 1

DESTRUCTIVE ANGER

In a controversy the instant we feel anger we have already ceased striving for the truth and have begun striving for ourselves.

~ Siddhārtha Gautama (Buddha)

When the part of the brain that is responsible for the survival of the being is in command, it blocks the ability to connect with the inner wisdom. It is focused on being right and winning. The tendency is to become self-centered and, in a debate, bring forth arguments that confirm and validate the points being made and show how the opposing party is wrong. The conversation in the head goes like this: "One of us is going down, and it ain't me."

When the anger shows up and it is not dealt with in healthy ways, the conversation changes quite rapidly into a fight, in which there can only be one winner. Strong thoughts of righteousness combined with extreme egocentrism only feed and fuel the fire of anger even more.

HEALING PATH:

During a conversation with someone, notice the moment you feel the anger, STOP and assess the intensity. If you notice that you are just fighting to be right, then remove yourself from the interaction and bring yourself back to calmness. Once calm and centered, make use of assertive communication; it values the right for both parties to express their thoughts and words in a calm and respectful manner. There is no need to be a passive pleaser or an aggressive attacker. Here are the steps to use in assertive communication (based on Marshall B. Rosenberg):

1. "When…" – Describe the situation – no blame, simply narrate the facts as you see them.
   Example: *When you yelled at me…*

2. "I feel…" – What feelings are brought out due to the situation above?
   Example: *I felt angry.*

3. "Because…" – Give your reasons.
   Example: *Because I believed I was being attacked, and I needed to defend myself, to end the argument.*

4. "Could we…" – Offer a solution, which the other person can accept or make a counter offer, until a solution is reached that both people can abide by.
   Example: *Could we talk another time when we are calmer?*

Anger is a stone cast into a wasp's nest.

~   Pope Paul VI

Once angry words are said, or angry actions are executed, there is no control of how the target of these words or actions might react. The echo of your behavior can come back multiplied and intensified. The wasps that initially were just going about their business may now be infuriated. While they might be smaller in size, they win in numbers.

Everybody has the right to their anger, and the anger might even be justified for the situation. Maybe one of the wasps bit you and it hurts badly. Still, it is better to pause for a bit, before reacting out of pain.

HEALING PATH:

1. Give people the benefit of the doubt. Most people do not wake up with a plan to hurt other people. Most people are just trying to survive, live, and find a sense of peace and safety in the world. If they knew better, they would do better. Maybe you got too close to the wasps' nest and they were just protecting themselves. Maybe they were already in an angry mood before you came along, and your stone was the cherry on the angry cake.

2. Before throwing the stones, try practicing "the throw". Write down what you would say, put it aside, sleep on it, and review it the next day, when the pain of the sting is no longer as strong. Tape yourself saying it and then listen to the recording, pay special attention to the tone of your voice. Or have a friend stand in for the other party and express your frustration with a neutral person and be open to their feedback.

3. Examine your own "anger issues". What is it that blinds you to the potential consequences of throwing anger at a dangerous target? Are you being reckless, innocent, naive or you just don't know better?

I am not as angry as I used to be. But I can get in touch with that anger pretty quickly if I feel my space is being invaded or somebody is not treating me with the respect that I think I want.

~ Samuel L. Jackson

This quote could be alluding to three aspects of anger: anger intensity, anger control and the connection between anger and respect.

The first aspect speaks to the ability to change the intensity of anger over time. It seems that maturity might have an impact on the ability to gage the intensity of anger and that the intensity of the anger is something that can be controlled.

The second aspect in the quote, touches on the capacity to conjure up anger voluntarily and quickly if needed. This piece points to the choices available to us: to let the anger take hold of you, or not!

The third aspect that this quote refers to, is how the level of anger is connected to a personal definition of respect. There are some universal concepts on what respect means, yet there are also nuances that are unique to each individual. What one person considers to be respect might not match up with how another person defines the concept of respect.

HEALING PATH:

Here are some thoughts that can help create your personal definition of respect:

- I feel respected when...
- I feel disrespected when...
- I think I am respectful of others when...
- I think I am disrespectful to others when...
- People should or should not...
- I should or should not...

Once you are clear on what it means to be treated with respect, communicate this in an assertive manner to the people around you, to prevent future misunderstandings

Words can be said in bitterness and anger, and often there seems to be an element of truth in the nastiness. And words don't go away, they just echo around.

~　Jane Goodall

Words can be like seeds and sometimes even the seeds of anger and bitterness can grow stronger out of the pain. Why do people express anger and bitterness? Because that is reflective of the emotions that are currently active in the individual.

When emotional suffering is happening, the moral and mental filters tend to be momentarily inaccessible, because the focus is on the strong emotions. This in turn can lead to a brutal and unfiltered expression of these emotions through words and actions, without any awareness of the consequences and pain that this strong expression might cause. Many times, there is no intention to hurt, yet it does.

HEALING PATH:

Before expressing yourself in person, or in writing, ask the following questions.

1. Is it a good time—both for me and the other person—to express myself?

2. What emotion am I feeling, and do I want that emotion be reflected in my tone?

3. What is my intent, and are my words in accordance with the desired outcome?

In other words: Is the TIMING right, is my TONE kind, and is my CONTENT true, necessary, and relevant

A broken bone can heal, but the wound a word opens can fester forever.

~ Mary Jessamyn West

I cannot count the amount of times that I have had clients come to a session and repeat back to me hurtful words said by their partners. The words were spoken days, weeks, months or even years before, yet still echo in my clients' minds and hearts. These words created deep wounds, and as they keep being remembered the wounds keep oozing resentment, anger, and other painful emotions.

How words are said can have a big impact. Another anonymous quote that reflects that well is, "Say what you mean, mean what you say, don't say it mean." I believe that words carry energy. There are some anecdotal experiments on the negative effects of harmful words on water and plants.

HEALING PATH:

To undo the hurt caused by hurtful words try one or both options below:

1. Giving an honest, sincere apology. This requires that the person apologizing is able to fully empathize with the pain of the wounded person. That empathy walk in the wounded person's shoes can only be done once the speaker is willing to take off their own shoes, i.e. get out of their own mindset of being right, win the argument or wanting to defend or justify themselves.

2. Once a heartfelt apology has been made, the recipient of the apology, the wounded one, needs to be able to fully accept the apology and let go of the words said previously. Stop the mind every time it tries to bring the hurtful words back. Simply, truly delete that option from the mental system. Easier said than done, I know. But not impossible. It requires awareness and a true and serious desire to let go of the habit of replaying and reliving in your mind the painful memory over and over again. It gives you de opportunity to be the master of your mind and not be controlled by it.

Holding on to anger is like grasping a hot coal with the intent of throwing it at someone else; you are the one who gets burned.

~   Siddhārtha Gautama (Buddha)

For anger to be felt, it must first be generated. The anger fire is composed out of a potentially lethal combination of thoughts, hormonal juices, and other emotions that prepare the body for action. The body pumps up and is ready to defend the self or attack, for what feels like an impending war.

What happens though, if the target of the anger is no longer available? They either left, they are taller, bigger, smarter, or the environment (office place, store, etc.) is not appropriate to express your anger and detonating it might have dire consequences.

Now the expression of anger has been thwarted and the pent-up energy is creating havoc and lots of damage to the human system. The cost of suppressed anger is high. It has negative effects on the mind, the psyche and the body.

HEALING PATH:

When you notice that anger is starting to rise, try to use the following formula (based on Jack Canfields' formula) to evaluate the costs:

S + R + T = C

Situation = Describe the anger-triggering situation. Do you have control over it? (Nine out of ten times we do not have much control.)

Response = R stand for response, better than reaction. Reacting is immediate, responding involves thinking, conscious evaluation and choice.

Timing = Is this a good moment to respond? Maybe it is better to wait for a better occasion?

Conclusion = Will depend on the result of the sum of the previous variables.

You cannot get ahead while getting even.

~ Dick Armey

Imagine you are climbing a mountain with the goal to get to the top, and you continually stop along the way to spend your energy fighting. Maybe you feel frustrated with the slow progress or lack thereof, with uncooperative people or people that get in your way. You then decide to fight and realize that this releases your frustration and activates adrenaline and cortisol, which in turn serve as fuel for the climb.

The metaphor above illustrates how life sometimes goes for us. We are trying to succeed in life, we get frustrated, we unleash the anger onto others and that gives us new "fighting energy".

The problem with this pattern, is that your body will crash once the adrenaline wears off, requiring some rest and restore time. Like the above quote suggests, you won't make it ahead—you won't arrive at your desired destination—when you're expending your energy in getting even.

HEALING PATH:

Anger can be channeled to propel the journey ahead and at the same time to strengthen resiliency.

1. Think of a situation that recently brought up your anger. Replay the situation in your head like a movie and at the same time notice how it feels in your body. How does the anger rise? Where is it created and located in your body? Are there specific qualities or other emotions linked to the anger?

2. Once you have a clear perception of the above, remember the first time you felt that exact kind of anger, way back into your younger years. Many of my clients report connections to impactful family dynamics somewhere between the ages of 5 to 10.

3. When the "original anger-provoking situation" is identified, it shows the "original wound". The reason you get angry in the situation described above is because the original wound is not healed yet.

4. Now answer the following question: If you could go back in time, what would you tell your younger self or do, during the "original anger-provoking situation" to prevent, avoid or minimize its impact? Once you have the answer, come back to the present and apply that solution to the current situation. The more you act in this "new way" the better you will get at it, healing the past wound and avoiding the rewounding.

For every minute you remain angry, you give up sixty seconds of peace of mind.

~ Ralph Waldo Emerson

An average 90-year lifetime has 2.838.240.000 seconds. People rarely are angry for just 1 minute. The time spent being angry depends on many factors. Personality, the anger-triggering issue, previous experiences, and level of resilience, to name a few. It can last 5 minutes (300 seconds) to a lifetime.

Anger is a normal human emotion that has its purpose. It is a strong emotion and difficult to control, yet not impossible. Controlling the reaction to an anger-eliciting situation can be learned and practiced. Do you want anger, or do you want peace?

HEALING PATH:

Try using the Awareness, Acceptance, Choice, and Change – AACC ©Model (which can be found on my website www.lifespects.com)

Awareness – Become aware of the anger. How, where, why does it manifest? Is it pure anger or are there other emotions? mixed in it? When did it start?

Acceptance – Accept the anger. Validate it. Why does it make sense that you are feeling angry?

Choices – Brainstorm different responses. How would a friend react in the same situation? How about someone that you respect? Choose what would be the best response.

Change – What needs to change so that peace of mind can be restored and remain? Is it an internal change on how you act or an external change that involves a larger system? Do you have enough resources to make that change?

> *Five enemies of peace inhabit with us— avarice, ambition, envy, anger, and pride; if these were to be banished, we should infallibly enjoy perpetual peace.*
>
> ~ F. Petrarch

There are many other enemies of peace that inhabit us, such as jealousy, rage, resentment, and so forth. All these enemies are there for a reason. The reason is that they need attention. They carry messages. Once the message is heard and the reason for their existence is understood, they can encourage growth, reduce and even remove the negative effects they carry with them.

Attempting to live in a place and space of love and peace, free of these five enemies, is a great goal to strive towards.

HEALING PATH:

One way to eliminate the "enemies" is to flood ourselves with qualities and emotions that bring strength and peace. This can be done by using the theory of flow (Mihály Csíkszentmihály). A state of "flow" is achieved when there is enough confidence and skills to perform a task that also provides a certain level of challenge. Being in "flow" provides a strong focus, and feelings of high energy and joy. Imagine an artist lost in their work. "Flow" is felt when a task is performed wholeheartedly, with spirit and soul, and when the motivation is fueled purely by intrinsic purposes instead of external rewards. Find your flow:

1. Which activity makes you lose sense of time, your surroundings and even your own basic needs?
2. When is your ability to concentrate intensely and maintain a strong focus at its peak?
3. When are you merged in action and awareness?
4. When do you feel in control of an activity?
5. When do you get a sense of immediate reward and gratification out of an activity?
6. Which activity gives you a feeling that you have the potential to succeed beyond your wildest dreams and expectations?
7. Does the activity have a clear set of goals and progress?
8. During this activity do you enjoy doing your best and do you feel that at the same time, you are contributing to something beyond yourself.

CHAPTER 2

ANGER
AND
THE BODY/BRAIN

Generally speaking, if a human being never shows anger, then I think something's wrong. He's not right in the brain.

~ Dalai Lama XIV

What does "never showing anger" mean? Does it mean to clench teeth, and stay quiet? Does it mean to show it, by being assertive? Or does mean that anger is suppressed and let out later in the form of passive-aggressive behavior?

What does it mean "not to be right in the brain"? Who is right in the brain? Whose brain is right and whose is not? Who determines what is a right brain? Does not showing anger mean that humans have evolved to a higher, more civilized state of being? Or is it the mark of a sociopath, or psychopath?

Even though the general meaning of this quote is understood, it ends up raising more questions than answers.

What this quote might be referring to is that anger is an emotion like any other. It is part of being human, to get angry is normal. What causes trouble is HOW anger is expressed.

HEALING PATH:

Finish the following statements to increase your awareness and knowledge about your anger:

1. What triggers my anger is…

2. When I get angry, I usually react by…

3. The reason I react in the way describe above and not in another way is because…

4. What brings me out of my anger is…

5. Sometimes I wish I could express my anger like… (Name a person that expresses anger in a healthy manner in your view.)

I am too weary to listen, too angry to hear.

~ Daniel Bell

Not being at our best physically can affect our mental resiliency. There is a Latin saying that goes like this: "Mens sana in corpore sano", a healthy mind needs a healthy body. When anger arises, it requires extra energy to fight the fight, and once the battle is won or lost, the body starts crashing. There is a sense of feeling tired and exhausted, and no energy is left to be attentive, caring, or compassionate.

In turn, the ability to listen and genuinely stay present when other people express their anger decreases, as does the capacity to stay tolerant in the light of information that might go against the belief of the listener.

Listening is an important aspect to the process of communication, and active empathic listening can increase the chances that anger will be dealt with in a healthy manner. However, to be a good listener, physical and mental energy is required to remain focused.

HEALING PATH:

The trick to be a great listener is to put aside the self. Imagine an external brain into which all assumptions, beliefs, expectations, shoulds and should nots could be downloaded into. Once released from inner filters, it is easier to activate the capacity to be open, curious, empathic, and genuinely interested. From that state, the following steps will better the act of listening:

1. Try to reflect back what the speaker is saying. (Use their words. This will increase feelings of being understood in the speaker and it will help in understanding better how the speaker thinks.)

2. Show interest by asking questions that start with what, who, when, where, how and why.

3. Do what therapists do and ask: How did that make you feel? Or simply say: Tell me more!

A hungry man is an angry one.

~ Buchi Emechta

There is some truth to the above quote. According to Abraham Maslow (American psychologist), there is a hierarchy of needs for all humans. This hierarchy starts with a human's basic physiological needs all the way up to the need to self-actualize. According to him, only when the needs on one stage are fulfilled can attention be given to the next one. Food is part of the first human need. No food, no fuel, no life. No wonder that it is hard to be nice when hungry!

HEALING PATH:

How to fulfill the needs in the hierarchy according to Maslow:

1. **Physiological needs**: Eat healthy nutrients, get good sleep and exercise regularly.

2. **Safety needs**: Have a safe shelter, a place that feels like home.

3. **Love and belonging**: Love yourself first, then share the love with another. In addition, find your tribe or tribes, people with shared common interests.

4. **Esteem**: Get trained, learn skills, and do work that is meaningful to you, that sparks your spirit, that utilizes your talents. This gives a sense of self-respect, confidence, and achievement.

5. **Self-actualization**: Create harmony, genuine understanding and non-judgment of yourself and others. Work on realizing you best potential. Surpass your own expectations, become better than you ever imagined.

Anger is brief madness.

~ Horace

It can be. What was considered madness during Horace's time is now considered mental illness. There are different diagnoses that have anger as one aspect of their symptomology, such as attention-deficit/hyperactivity disorder (ADHD) anger, anxiety anger, borderline personality anger, and post-traumatic stress disorder (PTSD) anger, to name a few.

Each one of these diagnoses have a specific set of symptoms, and their anger style differs. Sometimes the anger is part of the illness and sometimes it is about being diagnosed with a mental illness.

HEALING PATH:

Therapy, natural treatments, nutrition and/or medication are some options in the treatment of anger:

1. There are therapeutic techniques that have been researched and shown great results, such as Dialectical Behavior Therapy (DBT) to treat borderline personality disorder or Eye Movement Desensitization and Reprocessing (EMDR) for PTSD. A well-trained counselor can provide high-quality treatments.

2. Natural treatments might include minerals and vitamins. It has been shown that copper and/or iron imbalance in the body can influence anger, and Omega-3 helps decrease levels of anger. A naturopathic doctor is the best person for this route.

3. Certain foods can increase or decrease our propensity for aggressive behavior. A nutritionist can be of great help.

4. Certain psychotropic drugs have been shown to reduce the levels of anger. A psychiatrist could assist in developing a medication regimen and treatment plan, based on a thorough assessment.

5. Hallucinogenic medicines are being used to treat some mental illnesses and their symptoms. It is called psychedelic assisted therapy. Legal aspects of these medicines should be considered.

It is advisable to consult professionals before making a choice of treatment.

> *My body is damaged from music*
> *…I have an irritation in my*
> *stomach. It's psychosomatic, caused*
> *by all the anger and the screaming.*
> *I have scoliosis,…I'm always in*
> *pain, and that adds to the anger in*
> *our music.*
>
> ~ Kurt Cobain

Even though the quote does not talk about addiction, it is known that the author suffered from it. Substance abuse requires attention. Not all drugs are bad, and some can help expand consciousness. Mind-altering substances become a problem when they start destroying one's body, career, relationships, or life in general. Addiction is self-medication from pain. The more self-medication is done, the less the pain is addressed and the bigger the hole gets. The treatment steps are simple; the execution of the steps, not so much. To heal, the addictive substance needs to be removed, the pain needs to be looked at, the ability to deal with negative emotions strengthened, and the hole in the soul needs to be filled with love and compassion. When substance abuse causes trouble, substance abuse is the trouble. There is a saying that goes: "The person takes the drug, the drug takes the drug, the drug takes the person."

HEALING PATH:

The solution is to get high on life, be compassionate with the self, and find a meaningful path that nurtures the soul.

Answer the following questions based on the 12-steps program of Alcoholics Anonymous (AA) and Narcotics Anonymous (AA):

1. Are you ready to admit to the problem?

2. Are you willing to surrender to a higher power for help?

3. Are you willing to look at and get in touch with the pain deep inside?

4. Are you prepared to make amends with the people you have harmed?

5. Are you ready to admit to any wrongdoings and to be honest with yourself and others?

6. Will you continuously strengthen your bond with the higher power?

7. Are you excited to feel awakened and ready to live life in full and help others in need?

CHAPTER 3

ANGER
AND
PARENTING

We're taught to be ashamed of anger, fear and sadness, and to me they're of equal value to happiness, excitement and inspiration.

~ Alanis Morissette

Emotions are messengers. The so called "good ones" like joy, happiness, excitement and inspiration are desired and welcomed to stay forever. The so called "negative ones" like anger, fear and sadness tend to get suppressed or denied. The reality is that every emotion has a meaning and a purpose.

The reason, for instance, that anger is felt, is because there is a situation that doesn't seem "right" or "fair" according to each person's perspective. Fear is generated when a situation that is new or dangerous arises and there is no strength or confidence to face it. Last, but not least, sadness is felt when we go through a major undesired life change or some form of loss happens.

HEALING PATH:

Emotions are a package deal; you either feel all of them or none. Below are three steps to increase emotional intelligence.

1. Recognize your emotions and name them, for instance: "I am feeling leery/giddy/glad" (a list of emotions can be found in an internet search).

2. Accept that all emotions are normal and that you created the emotion. No one can "make" you angry; only you can do that.

3. Listen to the message from the emotion:
    - Why am I (e.g. angry)?
    - What does that mean to me?
    - How should I handle this?
    - Who can help?

Allowing children to show their guilt, show their grief, show their anger, takes the sting out of the situation.

~ Martha Beck

Parenting has evolved. Once children were seen as little adults. Later people believed they were blank slates. These days, they are seen as vulnerable beings that have personality and deserve to grow and develop in a space of love, safety, and acceptance so they can fully discover who they are and find their own path to happiness.

Below is a list of dysfunctional roles children, based on Sharon Wegscheider's work (1981), tend to take on when they are punished for showing negative emotions, instead of being understood and receiving validation. Children need to learn that anger, guilt, grief and other so-called negative feelings are normal, and can be expressed. Parents should teach children how to self-soothe, and how to name and express those emotions in healthy ways.

HEALING PATH:

Which role do you identify with?

1. **The hero** — Is responsible, self-sufficient, perfect, rigid, and controlling, but makes the family look good on the outside.

The healed hero — Seeks healthy achievement instead of success at all costs; has learned to accept "good enough" instead of "perfection".

2. **The scapegoat** — Is the black sheep, the troubled one, impulsive and angry, also sensitive and caring, that child helps distracts from the real family issues.

The healed scapegoat — Learns to bring their sensitivity and caring to people that appreciate it.

3. **The caretaker** — Is kind, generous, meets everybody's needs, does not know how to take care of their own needs, they are the helpers.

The healed caretaker — Takes care of themselves first, before taking care of others, knows how to set healthy boundaries.

4. **The lost child** — Is ignored, invisible, daydreams, withdraws from the hard reality, they try not to bother.

The found child — Has learned to express their feelings, sometimes through creative endeavors, they are great listeners.

5. **The clown** — Is funny and makes others laugh to defend against feelings of inadequacy and vulnerability, often the youngest child.

The healed clown — Allows space of expression of all emotions and knows how to show vulnerability.

Words, especially when yelled in anger, can be very damaging to a child's self-confidence. The child probably already feels bad enough just from seeing the consequences of his or her behavior. Our sons and daughters don't need more guilt and self-doubt heaped upon their already wounded egos.

~ Jack Canfield

Children are like sponges, they absorb their environment with curiosity, eagerness, and vulnerability. Parents and adults are responsible for carefully choosing what kind of world they want to show their children, and which behaviors will be modeled.

When adults lose control and throw an adult temper tantrum, it should not be a surprise when children start acting in the same manner.

Eric Berne developed a clear and concise model of 3 main states of mind that a grown person can show themselves through: the child, the parent, and the adult. They all have their appropriate place and time to be expressed.

HEALING PATH:

These states described below are independent of biological age.

The child state can show up in 2 different types: (1) the free, happy, open, playful, creative, exploring, and vulnerable child; and (2) the adaptive child, that reacts and changes according to the environment around them to better fit in or that rebels, is insecure and throws tantrums.

The next state of mind is the parent state of mind, which also has 2 types: (1) the nurturing parent that calms, supports and provides a sense of safety and (2) the controlling, critical, patronizing parent.

The third state is the adult state, which does not need to control nor react. When in that state the individual is reasonable, logical, rational, non-threatening, and feels comfortable in themselves.

The different states are expressed through the choice of words, tones, gestures, postures, and facial expressions.

Start noticing when you have left your nurturing parent or adult state and have entered the controlling parent zone or even worse, reverted back into the tantrum-throwing child zone.

You've just got to have a sense of respect for the person you have children with. Anger doesn't help anybody. Ultimately you have to say forgiveness is important and honoring what you had together is important. But it's easy to say and harder to do.

~ Nicole Kidman

Divorce can be hard, and it rarely happens smoothly. Yet having a good divorce and creating a positive co-parenting alliance is not impossible; it can be done. Quite often anger gets in the way of creating a harmonious environment during divorce proceedings, and children tend to pay the ultimate price of parents running their personal agendas.

Children are resilient and they can adapt, as long as their caretakers act in an adult manner. When, during a separation and/or divorce, the adults are able to keep the well-being and interest of the children in mind, the negative consequences affecting the children can be diminished or even avoided.

HEALING PATH:

During divorce or separation proceedings *LEAVE THE KIDS OUT OF IT!* They did not ask for it, they shouldn't pick up the tab of adults misbehaving. Keep a respectful relationship with the person that *YOU CHOSE* to have children with!

For that check the messages inside your head and the ones you verbalize and make the following changes:

Instead of	Try saying
- **I have to** be nice…	- **I choose to** be nice…
- **I don't have to** respect…because…	- **I choose not to** respect…because
- **I have to** forgive…	- **I choose to** forgive…
- **I can't** get along…	- **I won't** get along…
- **I can** be mean…	- **I will** be mean….
- **I am afraid** we will never get along.	- **I would like/I look forward** to get along
- **I am unable to** control my anger.	- **I am unwilling to** control my anger.

Choose your own answers to the sentences above.

We come from fallible parents who were kids once, who decided to have kids and who had to learn how to be parents. Faults are made, and damage is done, whether it's conscious or not. Everyone's got their own 'stuff,' their own issues, and their own anger at Mom and Dad. That is what family is. Family is almost naturally dysfunctional.

~   Chris Pine

The upbringing people experience as children shapes them on a neurological and cellular level. It is imprinted in their brain, and as adults they operate out of that programing, most of the time unconsciously, unless they have done some deep examination to reach more awareness.

Changing the perception of the parenting given or making peace with a dysfunctional past is part of creating a harmonious, joyful and happy existence for yourself and others.

HEALING PATH:

One-way to heal childhood emotional wounds is to attract partners that exhibit traits that are similar to their caretakers. To start healing, instead of fighting those traits, use them to change your responses to them and expand your ability to be in the world.

1. Start by making a list of pros and cons of your parents or from the people that were the most impactful during your formative years.

2. Then pick out the 3 qualities that stuck out the most for you.
   E.g. My Mom was a cold and distant parent.

3. Write down how you would typically react to that trait as a child.
   E.g. Be sad and isolated and look for emotional connection with other people.

4. Then notice how these tendencies are present in your partner and in your current relationships.

5. Then decide to respond in an adult manner versus a 6-year-old manner.
   E.g. When you perceive (sometimes inaccurate) that your partner is being cold, instead of being sad, isolating and looking for others (your typical childhood response), talk to your partner and express what you are thinking and feeling, or…(come up with a more mature response for yourself).

CHAPTER 4

FEMALE ANGER

I have a right to my anger, and I don't want anybody telling me I shouldn't be, that it's not nice to be, and that something's wrong with me because I get angry.

~ Maxine Waters

#M etoo. Women have suffered from dysfunctional anger way too long. One reason women tend to suppress their anger is they fear that once the anger is expressed, they will be rejected and the relationship severed for good. Men don't worry much about this and socially it has been more acceptable and at times encouraged for men to show their anger overtly.

The difference in socialization among genders has resulted in limited opportunities for women and contributed to gender inequality. To regain equality, one of the skills that is important for women to learn and execute is the capacity to express anger in positive ways and set healthy boundaries. Women and men play a role in breaking the cycle of gender inequality. Usually if a woman expresses her anger directly, like a man would, she does not get heard, because there is an expectation for women to be tender, caring, maternal and "quiet". This might cause the woman to turn her anger inward, perpetuating an unhealthy cycle.

HEALING PATH:

Follow the steps below to start setting healthy boundaries. The first step in effectively setting boundaries is self-awareness.

Complete the following sentences using as many examples as you wish, thinking of situations in which you feel, have felt, or would feel violated:

1. People may not

_____.

Ex: People may not embarrass me in front of others.

2. I have a right to ask for

_____.

Ex: I have a right to ask for help.

3. To protect my time and energy, it's okay to

_____.

Ex: To protect my time and energy, it is okay to change my mind.

Because society would rather, we always wore a pretty face, women have been trained to cut off anger.

~ Nancy Friday

Suppression of anger often leads to negative results, such as depression and anxiety, self-harming behaviors, substance abuse and illnesses. The energy bound up in suppressing, inhibiting, and re-directing anger makes it unavailable for creative pursuits.

The dread of social isolation, disapproval and in some cultures even punishment, leads many women to suppress anger and avoid any type of assertive or competitive behavior.

There is a need for some gender-specific anger management treatments that are geared specifically towards women.

HEALING PATH:

Teresa Bernardez-Bonesatti, M.D., offered very valuable insight on how to assist women in dealing with their anger. The steps are listed below:

1. Have a supportive therapeutic environment for women in which anger can be expressed safely.
2. Receive reassurance and legitimization in the ability to experience one's own legitimate anger in the presence of tolerant and unfrightened witnesses.
3. Have coherent explanations, which takes deeply into account the role of social factors in inducing conflict.
4. Achieve an awareness of the intensity, source, and purpose of the anger. Only when women realize the sources of their strength and ability, can they afford to take risks.
5. Allow women to take up their own cause.
6. Become critical and develop the capacity to separate one's own feelings (while being aware of them) from the matter to be evaluated.
7. Assess and evaluate oneself and the outside world based on information and objective appraisals.
8. Practice in shared conflicts with other women.
9. Restore a state of well-being and creativity.
10. Regain self-respect.

A man who has never made a woman angry is a failure in life.

~ Christopher Morley

At times when a woman is angry it means she cares. Yet, the anger can be misinterpreted as being critical, which in turn might bring out a sense of shame in others, leading to the rejection of the care being shown through the anger. That rejection will in turn increase the female anger and perpetuate a vicious cycle. One way to get out of that unhealthy shame/anger cycle is to learn to communicate in a healthy manner. Harville Hendrix developed the Imago model that includes communication steps that lead to successful understanding. They are summarized next.

HEALING PATH:

1. Make an appointment to talk (what might be a good time to express yourself, might not be a good time for your partner).

2. Define who is going to be the speaker first and who will be the listener (later the roles are switched). Start with the MIRRORING step.

3. As a speaker, stick to one topic at a time and express you anger in the following way: "Sometimes what upsets me is…" Speak in paragraphs, 1 to 5 sentences.

4. The listener reflects verbatim, keeping a kind and compassionate tone. "What I heard you say is…", "Did I get that?", "Is there more?"

5. Go back and forth until the one topic is expressed in its entirety.

6. Now the listener SUMMARIZES what was heard in one paragraph and checks with speaker if correct.

7. The listener VALIDATES what makes sense. "It makes sense to me that you would feel this way… because (in listener's own words)." No defending on the part of the listener is needed.

8. The listener asks: "What can I do to help you feel less frustrated in this situation?"

9. The speaker offers 3 possible solutions, and the listener checks if any of the solutions can truly and honestly be fulfilled by the listener. If not, a counter solution is offered, and they go back and forth until a solution is found that both parties can agree on.

10. Speaker and listener switch roles and start on the same topic at # 3.

CHAPTER 5

ANGER

AND

OTHER EMOTIONS

Anger has a way of seeping into every other emotion and planting itself in there.

~   Dane Cook

There are many emotions that have a component of anger in them. Learning to identify and name the emotions that are present at any given time increases emotional awareness.

The practice of naming emotions not only increases emotional awareness, it increases emotional literacy as well and it decreases the energetic potency of that emotion. This is even more helpful in case of unpleasant emotions.

On the next page is a small sample of different combinations between anger and other emotions and concepts.

HEALING PATH:

- **Grief anger** – anger over the loss of a loved one
- **Empathic anger** – when anger is felt on behalf of someone else who is in a less fortunate position in life
- **Rejection anger** – results from feeling rejected, whether the rejection is real or imagined
- **Stress anger** – associated with the stress response, it is the emotion that elicits the fight-or-flight response
- **Guilt anger** – results from the assumption of having done something wrong
- **Shame anger** – anger about the shame associated with feeling flawed
- **Regret anger** – anger about something that has been done or should have been done in the past
- **Jealousy anger** – shows up when there is a threat to a relationship
- **Anxiety anger** – associated with the inability to control the anxiety
- **Constructive anger** – anger that motivates positive changes
- **Learned anger** – anger behavior that has been modeled during childhood
- **Hormonal anger** – anger related to hormonal imbalance
- **Addiction anger** – shows up during or after the use of mind-altering substances
- **Spiritual anger** – anger connected with loss or change of spiritual beliefs

People who are prone to anxiety are nearly always people-pleasers who fear conflict and…feelings like anger. When you feel upset, you sweep your problems under the rug because you don't want to upset anyone. You do this so quickly and automatically that you're not even aware you're doing it.

~   David D. Burns

There is a connection between anger and anxiety. Anger can be a symptom as well as a cause of anxiety. Initially anxiety-anger seems to be paradoxical, since anxiety is often associated with fear, and anger with bravery and courage, and the sense of helplessness brought forth by anxiety makes it hard to evoke anger. Yet anger can present itself as a reaction to the frustration with the difficulty to act that is brought forth by the anxiety and fear. Deep anger issues can bring out anxiety, and the worry about the inability to control the anger can lead to further surges of anxiety, creating a vicious cycle.

People in anger tend to take more action and minimize or ignore the risks and consequences, while anxiety tends to promote inaction and low-risk actions.

HEALING PATH:

Sometimes anxiety can change to anger, when enough anger-inducing ideas are presented and believed.

It has been shown that peaceful and loving images help reduce the levels of anxiety and anger. This reinforces the importance of learning to calm the mind as a way of lowering anxiety.

Visual guided meditation is a wonderful tool to lower anxiety and anger, especially images that provide a sense of emotional security and connection. These could be images that are suggested during a guided meditation, self-chosen images, images from past experiences, and images that evoke a sense of peace, calmness, tranquility, and emotional safety.

I know of no more disagreeable situation than to be left feeling generally angry without anybody in particular to be angry at.

~ Frank Moore Colby

This quote refers to the concept of blame. Anger can show up when there is a belief that someone used provocation on purpose. If there is uncertainty about what or who to blame, a sense of loss of control follows, combined with fear, anxiety, self-blame and a general sense of stress.

The anger is burning inside, without a target to direct the anger towards. If the provocateur is known, it is easy to blame, and channeling the anger into blame helps shift to a false sense of self-control. In the end, blame does not help, since it negatively influences the ability to control emotions.

HEALING PATH:

Virginia Satir, a renowned psychotherapist, developed 5 categories of communication that people resort to when in stressful situations. Which one is your default, and which one serves you better when angry?

1. **Blamer** – Finds fault, does not accept responsibility, hides behind feelings of alienation and loneliness, tends to be more likely to initiate conflict.

2. **Placater** – Is a pleaser, non-assertive, doesn't disagree, and seeks approval. Avoids conflict and worries about how they are perceived by others.

3. **Computer** – They are correct, proper, calm, rational and cold, they do not display emotions, they hide vulnerability and/or a firework of emotions.

4. **Distractor** – Seeks attention to compensate for feelings of loneliness or inadequacy, they use a range of emotions to avoid an issue or manipulate.

5. **Leveler/Assertive** – Can relate to all people, is flexible and establishes rapport before trying to influence; is assertive, has high self-esteem and strong values. The goal is mutual problem solving, coupled with a positive intention behind everything. The leveler has emotional balance and comes across as 'on the level', centered and factual.

Grab the broom of anger and drive off the beast of fear.

~ Zora Neale Hurston

There is a strong connection between anger and fear; both are part of our survival system. Anger tends to be a more accepted emotion, because it is associated with strength, whereas fear often represents weakness.

For some people there is a fear of getting in touch with their anger, since doing this might result in loss of control, which could unleash worse emotions and/or behaviors.

Sometimes the triggers for fear come from the inside, such as in cases of childhood abuse, after which continued issues of fear of anger, violence, coercion, and abandonment may perpetuate high-risk behaviors, interfering with the ability to gain knowledge and health services.

It has been found, that the more an emotion is feared, the stronger it will be. For example, if two people get into a dispute, the person with low fear of anger will experience frustration in the situation but will move on fairly quickly. However, a person who is afraid of losing control of the anger might experience the same initial frustration but, due to the increased fear of anger, they will become upset with the fact that anger is being felt or that someone is "making" them experience anger, which leads to a much longer and more taxing emotional experience.

HEALING PATH:

To lower our fear and drive off the anger it is paramount to increase feelings of emotional safety. There is a simple yet powerful technique to do that.

Get a piece of paper and a pencil, colored ones if you will. Empty your mind with some deep breaths and make a drawing of a time in your young life in which you felt emotionally safe. If you have a hard time finding one, just imagine a scene that would have made your younger self feel safe. Get lost in the experience of the drawing, turn off the analytical part of the brain and activate the creative and imaginative.

When you are done, you can reengage your right brain and start thinking about ways in which you can recreate the scene of your childhood in your current life. Adapt the experience and make those changes to bring a higher sense of feeling safe back.

> *Guilt is anger directed at ourselves—at what we did or did not do. Resentment is anger directed at others—at what they did or did not do.*
>
> ~   Peter McWilliams

Guilt is a feeling that results from taking responsibility for believing to have done something wrong, it is the result of de sum between self-anger and compassion. Guilt is often a learned response. Unresolved guilt can linger for years.

Guilt can exaggerate a sense of responsibility and increase levels of sensitivity. It can get in the way of noticing other important feelings and interfere in decision making. It can also be a motivator for change in your life.

Guilt is fed by irrational beliefs such as: "I am responsible for X's (fill in a name) happiness"; "If my kids fail in any way, it's my fault"; or "If I feel guilty, then I must have been wrong."

Others may play on feelings of guilt by feeding into the above beliefs that they will suffer greatly if you do not respond positively to their request(s), even when it means violating your rights. They may accuse you of misdeeds, words, or actions to make you believe you are the one with a problem (this effectively takes the pressure off of them).

HEALING PATH:

Follow the steps below to alleviate feelings of guilt:

1. First identify the **pain** that is related to the feelings of guilt: "I feel guilty because_____."

2. Reflect on **responsibility**. Whose responsibility is it in the situation?

3. Reflect on **motivation**. What is the reason for the situation to have happened the way it did?

4. **Change,** if the responsibility is on you, or **accept** it, and move on.

5. Analyze the **use** of feeling guilty. What is the Point of feeling guilty? Is there a payoff to keep nurturing the guilt?

6. **Forgive** yourself and/or others.

7. **Reality check** with others that you trust.

8. Use **positive affirmations** to counteract the irrational negative beliefs.

9. Reflect on **parenting** received. Just because you were taught to feel a certain way, does not mean that it was accurate or valid.

Anger will never disappear so long as thoughts of resentment are cherished in the mind. Anger will disappear just as soon as thoughts of resentment are forgotten.

~ John Dryden

Resentment is unresolved anger, and one way that anger stays unresolved is by ruminating over the anger-provoking event over and over. Rumination keeps the focus on the negative mood, and the past negative experience keeps being replayed over and over in the mind. Rumination exacerbates the intensity and duration of anger, making it worse; it increases the level of psychological distress and aggression. Rumination inhibits anger from dissipating. The brain is stuck in a closed loop, preventing the creation or realization of healing or solution-oriented thoughts.

The online world can serve as fuel for the anger in the rumination loop. When past comments are reviewed, and interpreted as being provocative, there might be an increase in rumination and in aggressive responses.

HEALING PATH:

To get out of the rumination loop:

1. Distract your mind by singing a song, praying, reading or listening to something funny or engaging in positive interactions.

2. Stop the train of thought by thinking: "Stop." You might even visualize a big stop sign in your head.

3. Allow for rumination, schedule a time to start and end and ruminate like crazy during that time, and then stop when the time is up.

4. Talk to someone such as a trusted friend, a chaplain, or a therapist; sharing what is on our minds helps gain perspective and clear things up.

5. Do some journaling; it is like talking on paper.

6. Solve a small problem or accomplish an easy goal. Doing so will bring your mind back into a more positive state.

7. Are there any patterns? Do certain people, times or events increase your rumination?

8. Meditate.

Whatever is begun in anger ends in shame.

~   Benjamin Franklin

The connection between anger and shame is strong. Shame has its roots in our past, at a time where the child was made to feel deficient, inadequate, and unlovable. Brené Brown defines shame as "the intensely painful feeling or experience of believing that the person is flawed and therefore unworthy of love and belonging; something that has been done, failed to be done or experienced, makes the individual unworthy of connection." As a result, unhealthy coping mechanisms are developed to deny, suppress or alleviate feelings of shame. Some of these mechanisms are: expressing anger or contempt, withdrawing, blaming, controlling, being perfectionists and people pleasers.

HEALING PATH:

Here are strategies to help heal feelings of shame.

1. **Heal the inner child** – From an adult perspective, find the origin of your shame and realize that whatever happened was not your fault.

2. **Recognize triggers** – Notice what triggers your feelings of shame.

3. **Use self-compassion** – Treat and talk to yourself with the same kindness and love you show a valuable friend or a beloved, cherished child. Compassion releases oxytocin, which increases trust, calm, safety, emotional stability, and connectedness.

4. **Examine your thoughts** – Do not believe all thoughts; try to find evidence for and against the thoughts. Notice and reframe your negative thought patters around situations that trigger shame.

5. **Accept the shame** – Accept the shame as it comes, like a visitor that needs attention, love, and care. Do not add other negative emotions to it.

6. **Release people** – You can decide with whom you want to be. Choose emotionally healthy and caring, supportive, understanding, and loving people. Release people with toxic and dysfunctional behavior.

7. **Accept love and kindness** – Sometimes shame can create a shield that deflects love and kindness. Learn to let those in, openly and with gratitude.

8. **Forgive** – Forgive the people that shamed you. Only you can release them from inside of you. People are flawed. Trust that you know how to forgive and will learn to protect yourself from them.

> *Anger is just a cowardly extension of sadness. It's a lot easier to be angry at someone than it is to tell them you're hurt.*
>
> ~   Tom Gates

Especially for men, anger seems easier in many ways, because it generates energy, as opposed to sadness, which might trigger tears. Sadly, tears are still viewed as being weak. Socially, anger is still seen as a *male* and sadness as *female* emotion.

In term of the interplay between the anger and the sadness, many choose anger to cover up the sadness. Yet anger causes a bigger depletion in our emotional system than sadness. A less know fact is that, ultimately too much anger can lead to depression (when our system has nothing else to give anymore, it is depleted).

Additionally, another aspect in which anger and sadness interplay is in the resolution for the causes of these strong emotions. By covering the sadness with anger, the opportunity to go to the root of the problem is diminished, because the focus now is on winning the argument or getting revenge.

HEALING PATH:

Use the www.thetappingsolution.com, developed by Roger Callahan, for your own energy and healing power.

1. Identify the problem you want to focus on.
2. How do you feel right now? Rate it (0 low/10 high).
3. State: "Even though I… (describe the issue), I deeply and completely accept myself."
4. Tap the outer edge of the hand, on the opposite side from the thumb, while repeating the statement three times aloud. Take a deep breath!
5. Use firm but gentle pressure. Tap with 2 or 4 fingertips.
6. Tap 5–7 times each on the other eight points, repeating the statement.

- At the center/top of the head, with all four fingers.
- At the inner edges of the eyebrows.
- At the area between the eye and the temple.
- At the area under the eye, on the cheekbone, beneath the pupil.
- At the point centered between the bottom of the nose and the upper lip.
- At the point between the lower lip and the chin.
- Tap just below the hard ridge of your collarbone.
- On your side, about four inches beneath the armpit.
- And back where you started. Outer edge of hand.

7. Take a deep breath! Focus on the issue and rate it again. Keep doing rounds until it is "0".
8. You can install positive feelings (such as: "I enjoy the calm and peace that I have") using the same tapping points and sequences above.

Usually when people are sad, they don't do anything. They just cry over their condition. But when they get angry, they bring about a change.

~ James Russell Lowell

Sadness drains energy and brings us down, anger fires us up initially. One way to move from sadness to anger is first, allow for a good cry, hopefully in the company of someone who is loving, caring and empathic. Then start looking into what brought on the sadness in the first place and check if there is some pent-up anger that can be brought forth. Once the anger-triggering reason is found, then explore ways in which changes can be made to get out of the sadness-anger cycle. The model below, adapted from the change model proposed by James Prochaska and Carlo DiClemente, can be followed to implement these changes.

HEALING PATH:

Below is an adaptation of the model that leads to lasting change.

1. **Contemplation** – At this stage there is a desire to change and some vague direction on the final goal. This can be a time of excitement, but also anxiety. If the anxiety is too strong it might lead people to jump the next 2 steps and move into action right away, to feel a release from the anxiety, only to look back later and realize how vital the 2 steps in between are.

2. **Exploration** – At this stage the goal is to gather information that is related to the change. No analyzing, judging, or evaluating, simply collecting data, the more the better. Brainstorm possible options and scenarios.

3. **Preparation** – At this stage the goal is to start weeding out the useful from the non-useful. Start organizing the data from the previous stage. Eliminate what does not "feel" right, use your intuition and gut level as well, to make the decisions, until you have narrowed it down enough to move to the next step.

4. **Action** – Once you have honed into one choice, it is time to act. Make your move and start shifting toward the goal established in the last step.

5. **Maintenance** – Now is the time to maintain the new established change until a new change comes into play.

> *Boredom, anger, sadness, or fear are not 'yours,' not personal. They are conditions of the human mind. They come and go. Nothing that comes and goes is you.*
>
> ~ Eckhart Tolle

Eckart Tolle addresses an interesting concept with this quote, namely that all our emotions are transient, they come and go. This is good news for the so-called negative emotions mentioned in the quote above, bad news for emotions like joy, love, peace and harmony, since they are also of impermanent nature.

Emotions are not who you are; they are messengers that provide great information about yourself. Observe emotions as they come and go—do not let them attach to you. Find the message they bring and let them go. Here, the emotion of boredom will be explored, since the other emotions will be looked at in more detail in other quotes.

Boredom is a mixture between feeling weary and restless, without a particular interest to channel that energy into. If not addressed, boredom can increase the use of toxic substances, contribute to feelings of depression or stress, and can interfere with academic or work performance. On the other hand, boredom offers an opportunity for greater self-reflection and the start of a creative process.

HEALING PATH:

The questions below will help you start listening more attentively to the message that boredom brings.

How does the boredom show up for you?

☐ As an unpleasant feeling?

☐ As a lack of stimulation?

☐ As a lack of motivation to change?

☐ As indifference?

☐ As uncertainty?

☐ As a restlessness ready for a change?

☐ As an apathetic energy with no desire to do anything?

☐ Other_____

For each option you checked follow up with: Why do you think that is? Keep digging until the point of clarity is found.

Anger is a manifestation of a deeper issue...and that, for me, is based on insecurity, self-esteem and loneliness.

~ Naomi Campbell

Yes, anger can be the manifestation of other deeper issues, and these deeper issues can be based on insecurity, lack of self-esteem, loneliness and a myriad of other aspects.

Increasing and strengthening self-esteem in ourselves and those around us, can have many positive effects. It increases the sense of emotional security, decreases feelings of loneliness, and make us less prone to anger triggers.

HEALING PATH:

To increase self-esteem, follow the below steps.

1. Draw a circle and divide it in as many pieces of the pie as there are areas and roles your life (i.e. family, work, money, spirituality, physical health, etc.). Think of all the areas in which you are active in your life, and all the different roles you have.

2. Next place a 0 in the middle of the circle and a 10 at the end of each piece of the pie.

3. Rate yourself in each area (0 = really bad, 10 = really great). Let's say in the friendship area, if you believe you are happy and have great nurturing friendships, give yourself a 10 and color the whole piece of the friendship pie. If you believe it is just a 5 then color half of the piece of the pie. Keep rating and coloring each piece of the pie. This will give you a visual understanding of how you are doing in the different areas of your life that matter to you.

4. Once done, take each piece of the pie that are less than a 10 and think about how you can bring it up one point. Let's say in the work/career area you gave yourself a 6. What does it take for you to feel that your work/career life is worth a 7?

5. Once you have a list of things that can increase your self-esteem in each area of your life, turn them into SMART goals, meaning goals that are Specific, Measurable, Attainable, and Realistic, and set a Timeline for accomplishment.

6. Finally, execute the goals and then reassess.

Revenge is often like biting a dog because the dog bit you.

~ Austin O'Malley

Revenge means trying to inflict injury in a person in return for an insult from that person or persons. It is anger that is directed at an individual or organization in order to 'get back at them' when there is a feeling of being wronged. It is fueled by obsessive thoughts, creates high levels of stress, and increases health issues in ourselves.

Some acts of revenge, when paired up with self-control, remain as desires buried in our minds or eventually get forgiven and forgotten. Other acts of revenge cross the mental boundaries and are acted out in vengeful behaviors.

Studies have found that talking about revenge releases dopamine (a feel-good hormone) in our brains and this in turn can be addictive. That is why people tend to ruminate for long periods of time over vengeful fantasies and acts, and have a hard time letting go.

HEALING PATH:

One strategy to get relief from feelings of revenge is using the ancient Hawaiian method of Ho'oponopono. It is a practice that facilitates forgiveness and reconciliation. It helps cleanse the mind from the addiction of thinking. Once you feel mental distress or thoughts of revenge, repeat the following four sentences in your mind or out loud until you feel a sense of release:

"Thank you"

"I love you"

"I am sorry"

"Please forgive me"

These statements encourage you to take 100% of responsibility for any given situation. Once self-responsibility has been restored, self-empowerment ensues. Then changes can be made to avoid future pain.

Initially there might be a certain dissonance between the affirmations and the event or person you are upset about. The sentences might not make sense, yet the more you say them the clearer it will get. Your mind will find reasons for why it makes sense to be grateful in this situation. For instance, it could mean that you are grateful for the experience, because it gives you an opportunity to learn and grow. "I love you" could mean you love you, and you are "sorry" for putting yourself through such pain and that you need to "forgive" yourself.

While seeking revenge, dig two graves—one for yourself.

~ Douglas Horton

Sometimes anger is kept hidden deep inside dark corners of the self, and when paired up with images of revenge it can become unbearable. I have seen my fair share of clients who, in not knowing how to deal with the revenge-anger, end up hurting themselves. Not only emotionally, but literally, physically hurting themselves, using self-mutilation to stop the pain.

Most of them are not attempting to commit suicide, even though for some it is the end result. Cutting and self-harm occurs due to some physiological and some psychological reasons.

Physiologically, when the body gets hurt, hormones are released that help the healing process, kind of natural anesthetics, which create a bit of numbness. That is why when some people lose a limb, they don't feel the whole pain, because the body is creating a natural shield, otherwise it would be excruciating.

Psychologically, once there is an external wound representing the internal pain, the focus shifts to the healing, because it happens naturally, and there is no need to "do" anything. Plus, a level of control restored, in which the wound can be reopened, deepened, or allowed to heal. It deflects attention from the inner pain—that cannot be controlled—to the outer wound, that is visible.

HEALING PATH:

To heal self-harm, start by making the emotional pain visible to a trusted person—maybe a family member, a friend, a spiritual guide, or a therapist. Share it with someone who is able to stand in the pain with you, free of judgment or criticism.

Depending on how long the self-harming behaviors have been going on, there might be a need for a treatment facility, because after a while an action that is repeated over and over becomes a habit and/or an addiction, which makes harder and harder to break.

More than anything, there is a need to learn skills on how to self-heal emotionally. This can be done at a therapist office and/or through spiritual practices, books and other teaching and therapeutic tools.

The opposite of anger is not calmness, it's empathy.

~ Mehmet Oz

Empathy is a powerful antidote for destructive anger. Empathy is the ability we have to understand and share someone else's experiences, feelings and emotions. People who use empathy tend to achieve higher levels of success at work and socially. It is hard to muster empathy while angry. To develop empathy, sometimes, empathy needs to be felt from others before it can be given back to the self. When irritated, frustrated or angry, it is hard to muster up empathy, because the mind tends to get into an egoic state, which means there is a strong focus on the self and a loss in the incapacity to consider someone else's feelings.

There is a positive way to combine empathy and anger, it is called: Empathic anger. Empathic anger shows up when people get angry on behalf of a less fortunate being. When someone else's plight can be felt, and energy can be mustered up to protect them, or save them from further pain. Helping others in need increases our ability to feel empathy.

Showing empathy towards someone that is angry can help this person decrease their feelings of anger.

HEALING PATH:

How can it be done?

First you listen the person who is angry, just listen, non-judgmentally.
Ex. "I am so angry that I don't get valued at work and I feel like I want to punch my boss."

Then reflect back the words and/or the emotions you have heard.
"You don't get valued at work and that makes you angry."
(Leave out the part that shows a destructive behavior).

Validate the anger by telling them which part of their plight makes sense to you.
"Makes sense that you feel angry; not being valued at work can certainly feel upsetting and frustrating." (Again, leave out the behavior, validate the emotion and chose words that represent a less strong emotion). Once they are calmer and more rational you can empower them and assist in finding a solution to their anger by asking:

What do you think you can do in this situation?
Celebrate their answer if it is healthy and constructive, if not go back to the beginning!

CHAPTER 6

ANGER
AND
PERSPECTIVE

There are two things a person should never be angry at, what they can help, and what they cannot.

~   Plato

So very true, because getting angry at what we cannot help will only increase levels of stress. It makes us feel out of control and powerless. Getting angry at what cannot be controlled means that reality is being denied. Suffering comes from the desire for reality to be different, to make the individual feel better. Additionally, getting angry at what *can be helped* is not productive either; better to understand what did not work and think about what could have been done differently, learn the lesson and move on.

This reminds me of Diana Nyad, a 64-year-old woman who swam from Cuba to Florida. Every time she felt stuck, instead of getting angry she would say to herself: "Find a way" and so she did, until her final destination

GOT ANGER?

HEALING PATH:

Use the "miracle question" from solution-focused brief therapy to help you get out of being angry and stuck to moving forward.

"Tonight, you will go to sleep, and in the middle of the night, when you are fast asleep, suppose a miracle happens and all the problems you have are solved just like that. But since the miracle happened while you were sleeping, nobody knows how it happened. When you wake up the next morning, how are you going to start discovering that the miracle happened? What else are you going to notice? What else?"

Give yourself a lot of time to think and envision this new state of being. Make it vivid, full of images and emotions, and write about it.

Create a vision board based on your answers.

Anybody can become angry, that is easy; but to be angry with the right person, and to the right degree, and at the right time, for the right purpose, and in the right way, that is not within everybody's power and is not easy.

~ Aristotle

To be able to know and do what the above quote from Aristotle describes would raise humanity to a higher level in its developmental path. The perfect anger is a great goal to be achieved. The perfect anger is determined by many different components—our personality, our history, and our beliefs, to name a few. What angers one person might not anger another. A small anger trigger for one person, might be a big one for another. To achieve perfect anger, it is important to understand your anger. One way to get to know your anger better is to understand how anger has been passed down the generations, genetically and from a modeling perspective. A tool that can help is the genogram. It is a representation of a family tree and helps understand hereditary and behavioral patterns. It is widely used in many different areas; for instance, in the medical field it helps determine the history of medical conditions in the family.

HEALING PATH:

To help you create your anger genogram answer the following questions. Even if you are not related to your family through genetics you can still derive a lot of value, in doing the genogram.

1. How far back does your family tree go?

2. Who can you ask for information about the family tree?

3. How did each member in the family tree handle their own anger?

4. How did they respond to anger?

5. Any significant anger-provoking events that are noteworthy?

Every day we have plenty of opportunities to get angry, stressed or offended. But what you're doing when you indulge these negative emotions is giving something outside yourself power over your happiness. You can choose to not let little things upset you.

~ Joel Osteen

Let the inner voice be stronger than the outer voices. Choose to listen to the voice inside of you, the voice that is kind and wise. Even when someone or something triggers and upsets you, you still have the choice to decide if you will let that emotion overcome you.

There are several "voices" inside our head: the loving voice, the critical voice, the mean voice, the guilty voice, the angry voice, and so forth. First acknowledge those voices and realize that they don't have to be in there and they don't have to talk to you the way they do. You are the master of all these different aspects inside of you. The way to start changing the voices that create upset, is to strengthen the ones that increase self-esteem, confidence and love inside of you.

HEALING PATH:

Start on the path to resiliency.

1. When you go to bed write down or think about your day and reflect on the people or situations you are grateful for.

2. Then zoom in to the moment that was the happiest for you, the highlight of your day. Bring the memory back to the present, very vividly. Tell it to someone or write about it.

3. Why did you choose that moment?

4. Finally, ask yourself, "What do I want for the next day?"

5. In the morning read about the intention that you wrote the night prior and confirm it or choose another intention for the day.

It is wise to direct your anger towards problems—not people; to focus your energies on answers—not excuses.

~ William Arthur Ward

To strengthen your ability to focus your anger toward answers, it is important to pay attention to fragmented thinking.

Fragmented thinking is thinking that has no logical connections. Notice when you have a hard time staying focused on what is relevant. Focus on what will help you solve the problem at hand, on what is pertinent and related. Undisciplined thinking is often guided by associations (this reminds me of that, that reminds me of this other thing, and so forth), it is nonlinear and irrational. Logical thinking is linear, organized and evidence based. It goes step by step ("if A and B are true, and B and C are true, then C must also be true").

HEALING PATH:

Ask yourself the following questions to help figure out what is relevant:

1. What is the central question?

2. Am I focused on the main problem or task?

3. How is this connected? How is that?

4. Does my information directly relate to the problem or task?

5. Where do I need to focus my attention?

6. Am I being diverted to unrelated matters?

7. Am I failing to consider relevant viewpoints?

8. How is my point relevant to the issue being addressed?

9. What facts are actually going to help answer the question?

10. What considerations should be set aside?

11. Does this truly bear on the question? How does it connect?

I get angry at a principle, not a person.

~   Norman Schwarzkopf

The above quote gives an excellent strategy to redirect your anger: to not take it personally and to focus on the factual aspects of the interaction. To be able to get angry at a principle instead of a person, it is important to increase your ability to be reasonable. One of the hallmarks of a reasonable person is the disposition to change one's mind when given good reason to change. Good thinkers want to change their thinking when they discover better thinking.

HEALING PATH:

Below find several strategies for becoming more reasonable.

- Notice when you are unwilling to listen to the views of others and are seeing yourself as right and others as wrong.

- During a disagreement are you able to say: "Of course, I may be wrong. You may be right."

- Practice saying in your own mind, "I may be wrong and I'm willing to change my mind when given good reasons."

- Ask yourself, "When was the last time I changed my mind because someone gave me better reasons for an opposing view than I had for mine?" (To what extent are you open to new ways of looking at things? To what extent can you objectively judge information that refutes what you already think?)

- Realize that you are being close-minded if you are unwilling to listen to someone's reasons, are irritated by the reasons people give you, and/or if you get defensive during a discussion.

- Complete the following statements:
   a. I realize I was being close-minded in this situation because...
   b. The thinking I have a hard time letting go is...
   c. Thinking that is potentially better is...
   d. This thinking is better because...

I don't like anybody to be angry with me. I'd rather have friends.

~ B. B. King

No doubt that this is a wonderful option in life, yet there is a risk here of becoming a people pleaser or even worse, a doormat. The reality is that someone else's anger is their business and out of anybody else's control. Most times than not, anger gets triggered unknowingly. The reasons why there is a desire not to "make" anyone angry, is that without anger lives tend to be more peaceful. If people are not angry at you, you do not have to deal with their anger. On the other hand, you might miss an opportunity to learn to respond constructively when caught in the line of the anger fire.

Our thinking plays an important role in how the anger can be escalated or deescalated.

HEALING PATH:

Check if you abide by any of the kinds of thinking that can disrupt the peace. *Often, I...*

☐ ...jump to conclusions and/or assumptions.

☐ ...fail to think about consequences of my words.

☐ ...fail to notice contradictions.

☐ ...accept inaccurate information.

☐ ...ask vague questions.

☐ ...give vague answers.

☐ ...ask loaded questions.

☐ ...ask irrelevant questions.

☐ ...answer questions I am not competent to answer.

☐ ...ignore information that does not support my view.

☐ ...use irrelevant or confused ideas.

☐ ...misuse words.

☐ ...ignore relevant viewpoints.

☐ ...fail to see issues from the other person's point of view.

☐ ...am unaware of prejudices.

☐ ...do poor problem solving and make poor decisions.

When you learn that a truth is a lie, anger follows.

~ Grace Slick

Lies are statements intended to mislead others. Omission is the same as lying; it means lying by omission. Most people lie in average 1.5 times during the day, men tend to lie more than women (Saad, 2011).

People lie to feel better, to show agreement with another person, to hide insecurities, to get approval, to spare other people's feelings, to please others, and to preserve their self-image. Yet the person lied to is left feeling angry after finding out that they have been told a lie.

A good liar is congruent in their verbal message and the nonverbal signals. Otherwise the lie is detected through 'emotional leakage' in the facial expression. Women tend to be better than men at detecting liars, because women tend to be better at reading nonverbal messages. This is why women can get so appalled when a man cannot detect her emotional state by looking at her facial expressions. Men often have not had the proper training to read nonverbal signals accurately.

HEALING PATH:

How to stop a liar:

- Write down the times the person has lied.
- Confront them privately, calmly, and kindly.
- Give them a chance to explain.
- Hopefully they accept responsibility, ask for forgiveness, or apologize.
- Understand that it might take a while for them to change lying behavior.
- If they do not accept responsibility, and keep lying or blaming you, you might have to decide how many more lies you are willing to tolerate and when it is time to distance yourself.
- You cannot change anybody if they do not want to be changed.

How to stop yourself from lying:

- Hold yourself accountable to a non-lying standard.
- Know that in the long run lying is exhausting, the truth is easier.
- Recognize that sooner or later the truth comes out.

I'm too mature to be angry.

~ Jesse Jackson

Sometimes maturity is just a matter of time and comes out of facing life's challenges and experiences. From an emotional and psychological perspective, maturity is the ability to respond to your environment in an appropriate manner. Maturity also encompasses being aware of the correct time and place to behave and knowing when to act.

Part of being mature enough is to be able to become the master of your anger, instead of having it rule you. It includes creating a life that facilitates the process of maturation. This can be done by changing the quality of your life and know that the quality of your life is directly affected by the quality of your thinking.

HEALING PATH:

Below is a list with some ideas on how to increase the quality of your thinking, leading to more functional living.

- Choose some friends that don't think like you, to challenge your own views.
- Question your relationships, identify the issues, have a heart to heart talk, or leave the relationship of necessary.
- Take responsibility for your unreasonable thoughts or actions.
- There are at least 2 sides to life, positive and negative. Which one do you want to focus on?
- Leave your comfort zone so you can learn and grow.
- Accept that in life you don't always get what you want, and instead of pouting, change direction, and try something else.

When you assume negative intent, you're angry. If you take away that anger and assume positive intent, you will be amazed. Your emotional quotient goes up because you are no longer almost random in your response.

~ Indra Nooyi

A high emotional quotient is what the Emotional Intelligence (EI) movement is all about. Emotional Intelligence is the capacity to recognize, discern and label your emotions and the emotions of others in an attempt to guide your thinking and behavior and adapt to the world to achieve your goals. Studies have shown that people with high EI quotient have greater mental health, strong leadership skills and higher job performance. Daniel Goleman popularized the concept of EI and he suggests 5 constructs that comprise EI.

HEALING PATH:

Answer the questions below to increase your EI.

1. **Self-awareness** – To know one's emotions, values, weaknesses, and strengths, and to see their effect on others. To use gut feelings to guide decisions.

a) How many different emotions can you name?

b) What are your strengths, weaknesses and values?

c) Can you distinguish between gut feelings and brain feelings?

2. **Self-regulation** – To control/redirect disruptive emotions and impulses. To adapt to changes.

a) How do you control/redirect strong emotions such as anger and fear?

b) When change is needed, what strategy do you use?

3. **Social skill** – To facilitate the interaction in relationships.

a) In social settings are you able to show genuine interest, ask open-ended questions and listen?

b) Can you offer unique and special compliments?

c) Do you have good manners?

4. **Empathy** – To consider other people's feelings when making decisions.

a) Which situations bring out empathy in you?

b) Can you spread the empathy to situations that are more challenging?

5. **Motivation** – Being driven to achieve for the sake of achievement.

a) What motivates you? When is your motivation at its peak? Why?

b) How do you motivate yourself, especially when you don't feel like it?

CHAPTER 7

CONSTRUCTIVE ANGER

I am sometimes sad when I hear the personal stories of Tibetan refugees who have been tortured or beaten. Some irritation, some anger comes. But it never lasts long. I always try to think at a deeper level, to find ways to console.

~ Dalai Lama

Thinking on a deeper level requires the motivation and desire to do so. If you focus your attention for a moment on the role that thinking is playing in your life, you may come to recognize that, in fact, everything you do, or want, or feel is influenced by your thinking. To become better at thinking, focus on how your mind "moves". This is the same way that accomplished athletes learn what to do with their bodies—through mental practice and feedback.

HEALING PATH:

Read and answer the below questions to help deepen your thought process in anger situations.

1. What is really going on in this or that situation?
2. Are they trying to take advantage of me?
3. Does so-and-so really care about me?
4. Am I deceiving myself when I believe that…?
5. If I want to do…, what is the best way to prepare for it?
6. How can I be more successful in doing…?
7. Is this my biggest issue, or do I need to focus my attention elsewhere?

Then analyze your own thinking pattern with the below questions.

1. What do you know about how you think?
2. Have you ever studied your thinking?
3. What do you know about how the mind processes information?
4. Where does your thinking come from?
5. How much of it is "good" or "poor" quality? How do you know?
6. How much of your thinking is vague, muddled, inconsistent, inaccurate, illogical, or superficial?
7. Are you in control of your thinking?

I realized that if my thoughts immediately affect my body, I should be careful about what I think. Now if I get angry, I ask myself why I feel that way. If I can find the source of my anger, I can turn that negative energy into something positive.

~   Yoko Ono

There is substantial research that shows how damaging it can be to store and feed negative emotions in our body long-term. Somatic practices are body-centered therapies that look at the mind and body connection. Somatic practices explore how psychological and emotional aspects are stored in our bodies and provide techniques for releasing and healing. Practitioners say that emotions and memories can be "stored" in any part of the body as energy blocks, tensions, and imbalances, generating unhealthy patterns.

HEALING PATH:

Learn below about some body-mind therapies.

Rolfing – A technique of deep tissue manipulation to release and realign the body, and to reduce muscular and psychic tension.

The Rubenfeld Method – A method of mind-body integration that aids in recovery from physical and emotional trauma, release of tension, improved ease of movement, pain management, and improved body image.

Ayurveda – The traditional Hindu system of medicine, which is based on the idea of balance in bodily systems. Using a special diet, herbal treatment, and yogic breathing.

Yoga – A Hindu spiritual and ascetic discipline that includes breath control, simple meditation, and the adoption of specific bodily postures.

Reiki – A Japanese technique for relaxation and stress reduction that also promotes healing. It heals the "life force energy" that flows through all of us.

The Alexander Technique – A method that works to change movement habits in our everyday activities. It helps to release unnecessary tension and discover a new balance in the body.

The Feldenkrais Method – A type of exercise therapy that reorganizes connections between the brain and body and improves body movement and psychological state.

In times of great stress or adversity, it's always best to keep busy, to plow your anger and your energy into something positive.

~   Lee Iacocca

Breaking through your anger, focusing on a positive goal or action, and staying engaged in something that you are passionate about, is a great way to reverse the destructive nature of anger.

The desire to learn how to cope with anger goes far back in history. Greco-Roman authors wrote about it. Pope Gregory I proposed the use of virtues to combat the deadly sins. In the case of anger or wrath the virtue that cures it is patience.

The philosopher Seneca wrote an ancient manuscript on the topic of anger around 40 BC, it is called "De Ira" (On Anger), and his intent was to free people from the vice of anger. Another philosopher, Plutarch, also wrote about the anger. His work is named "De Cohibenda Ira" (On Controlling Anger), and he wrote it around 100 AC.

HEALING PATH:

Below is a list of adapted strategies to cure anger, suggested by Seneca. Check off the ones that you already mastered and mark the ones that you might want to work on.

- ☐ Slow down your pace
- ☐ Forgive mistakes
- ☐ Compose yourself in the midst of anger or leave
- ☐ Know that small things can lead to anger
- ☐ Avoid "falling into anger" and allowing it to take over reason
- ☐ Strengthen your soul
- ☐ Avoid alcohol or drugs
- ☐ Before reacting in anger, listen to the other person
- ☐ Raise healthy, respectful kids
- ☐ Listen to music that calms you down
- ☐ Make mental readjustments—do not trust easily what others say and avoid losing your temper based on false judgments
- ☐ Avoid undue self-regard
- ☐ Do physical exercises, relax the face, and modulate the voice
- ☐ Choose friends who model healthy anger

It was anger more than anything else that had set me off, roused me into productivity and creativity.

~ Mary Garden

Anger, if well used, can serve as fuel that motivates change and/or creates something new. Carol McGinnis developed a model that teaches how to harness and store the energy of anger and turn it to a productive emotion. These are the steps described in her model:

1. An EVENT happens that is perceived as just or unjust. If the event is perceived as
2. JUST, the person can move directly to the step of
3. RESOLUTION.
4. If it is perceived as UNJUST, a negative emotion arises.
5. If the emotion is ANGER, there is energy being generated. This energy, in turn, should be channeled into identifying what has happened.
6. Once the IDENTIFICATION has been made, there are 2 choices to express the anger.
7. A POSITIVE CHOICE will move the person into an appropriate expression that provides them with a sense of control.
8. A NEGATIVE CHOICE can move the person into a sense of loss of control that might become self-perpetuating and self-defeating (e.g. depression, drug/alcohol abuse, violence, aggression, or suicide).
9. Either one of those choices will bring some CHANGE and a
10. RESOLUTION.

HEALING PATH:

Although both options bring about change, and resolution, the positive route offers more appropriate options for expressing anger in a productive and healthy manner.

To make better use of the model above answer the two following questions:

1. What are things that make me feel alive?

2. Why do I do not do them, or why don't I do them more often?

If you are patient in one moment of anger, you will escape a hundred days of sorrow.

~ Rainer Maria Rilke

Patience is the capacity to accept or tolerate delay, difficulty, or annoyance without getting angry or upset. Patience is the antidote to the sin of wrath. Impatience means lack of patience.

Impatience stems from wanting immediate gratification and the frustration that comes with not receiving that. Impatience has some benefits, such as motivating change to create better goals in life. On the other hand, it can be detrimental if our original goal is worth sticking to, and it gets switched instead of patiently pursued. Being impatient can lead to rash decision-making with terrible consequences. Being too patient, on the other hand, can lead to wasting vast stretches of life pursuing the wrong goals.

HEALING PATH:

You can learn what triggers your impatience and manage your emotions. You can also learn to measure your reactions. One way to increase your level of patience is a technique used in Neuro-linguistic programming (NLP), developed Richard Bandler and John Grinder and is combination of psychotherapy, personal development, and communication,

1. Think of a situation in which you felt very impatient and wished you could feel more patient. Get a clear picture of the moment when your impatience was really strong.
2. Now put that image aside in your mind.
3. Next think of a time when you felt super patient. Bring that time alive into your mind and zoom into the moment when the patience was at its highest. Notice how you are feeling in your body notice the thoughts you are having, flood yourself with the sense of patience.
4. While keeping that moment of patience alive, slowly bring back the image of the impatient situation. There might be an initial discomfort.
5. Let all that settle inside of you and notice if your response in the impatient situation would have been different, had you been able to stay patient inside instead.

This is like a transfusion of states. You can artificially bring to mind a good state, to deal with a situation that might not be easy. This might bring forth a more positive result.

It is important to feel the anger without judging it, without attempting to find meaning in it. It may take many forms. Life is unfair. Death is unfair. Anger is a natural reaction to the unfairness of loss.

~ Elizabeth Kübler-Ross

Elizabeth Kübler-Ross created the stages of grief to help people better understand their emotional process after a great loss. The anger that is part of the grieving process is an anger that is connected to that sense of not having control over the losses. Especially in the case of death, which is such a final loss, there is no chance of reversal. When someone passes away, it can lead to an emotional roller coaster that not only includes anger, but many other emotions even numbness when the pain is too overwhelming. The Stages of grief are:

1. Denial - I can't believe this is happening.
2. Anger – Why me? It's Not fair.
3. Bargaining – If I do x the situation can be reversed or mitigated.
4. Sadness and other emotions – I am sad, confused, embarrassed, feeling guilty, why strive?
5. Acceptance – Since I cannot change the situation, how do I strengthen myself? Everything's going to be okay.

HEALING PATH:

The best way out of the pain of grief is through it. It is a process; it has a clear beginning, not a clear ending, yet it can end. Once acceptance of the loss has set in, there are 2 strategies that can be of great help to release the pain of grief.

1. Find meaning in the loss. You do this by thinking of all the positives about the person who just passed or situation the changes and incorporate those into your own life. In that way, you honor their life, you let them live through you, and you become a better person along the way.

2. Write a goodbye letter to the person who passed or the situation that just changed (usually at this point, even my most stoic clients choke trying to hide the tears). In the letter include everything: why you are sad, all emotions you are feeling, why you will miss them, why you love or loathe them. If there is any unresolved business lay it out. This activity is a little harder than the first, but very healing.

CHAPTER 8

ANGER
AND
AWARENESS

My father was often angry when I was most like him.

~ Lillian Hellman

This quote refers to the concept of projection. Projection is a way of defending against inner unconscious impulses, desires, qualities and/or vulnerabilities. Those undesired aspects get denied and attributed to others, to then be judged as bad in other people. The reality is that those exact same qualities are buried deep within the person doing the judging.

People with strong narcissistic aspects to their character tend to use projection quite often. They tend to blame others even when it is clear that they are the ones in the wrong and responsible for their own suffering. What they are trying to hide is a strong sense of shame for not knowing how to act or for messing things up, because they expect total perfection in themselves. If by any chance they are caught in an undeniable mishap, they tend to react with extreme anger or even rage.

HEALING PATH:

Every time you have something to say about others replace their name with "I" and think about it. Below are some examples.

- He/she hates me. – I hate me, I hate him/her.
- He/she is so… (e.g. unreasonable). – I am… (e.g. unreasonable). Explore situations in which you might have been unreasonable and practice self-love.
- He/she is so critical of me. – I am so critical of me, I am so critical of him/her.
- Other people make me angry. – I make myself angry. How do I do that?
- Why don't they learn? – Why don't I learn? Why don't I teach?

Think about the examples you chose:

- Why does the converted sentence make sense?

- Can you find some proof that the conversion is true at times?

Let us not look back in anger, nor forward in fear, but around in awareness.

~ James Thurber

Looking back in time, has its benefits. It can assist in learning valuable lessons about past decisions. It is more beneficial, though, to do the past behavior analysis once the anger has subsided, otherwise it might taint the investigation in a negative way.

Looking forward is beneficial as well, if the intent is to create a future vision, and future goals. Fear can dampen and/or limit that process, by narrowing the focus of the mind into creating a safe and secure future, instead of allowing for creativity, challenge and growth to happen.

One way to create awareness that can propel you is by using the power of positive affirmations. Affirmations can neutralize and/or even replace the thoughts that generate and feed the anger and keep us stuck.

HEALING PATH:

Follow the steps below to create effective affirmations. The example below involves past anger and future fear. Let's say you are angry at a former partner that has betrayed you and now you are afraid of entering a new relationship out of fear of feeling the hurt of betrayal once again. Yet you long to have a new relationship without the anger and the fear.

While creating your affirmation pass it through the test of the questions below, stating it 3 times. Once in the first person "I", once in the second person "you", ideally while looking into a mirror, and once in the third person "he/she" or by using your name. Always with you in mind.

Example: "Every day I (you) (he/she/name) release(s) the anger and the fear, I (you) (he/she/name) actively engage(s) in therapy, reading and learning about healthy relationships, and I (you) (he/she/name) feel(s) whole and ready to start a loving relationship with a new partner."

1. Is the affirmation specific, true, action oriented and stated in the present?
2. Does it pass the acceptance test of the inner critic?
3. Can it be stated in the 1st, 2nd and 3rd person?
4. Why is that affirmation important? (This determines the motivation.)
5. How are you going to achieve it? (This defines the action steps.)
6. How will you feel once it comes true? (This determines the feeling attached to the new state you are seeking.)

When you are offended at any man's fault, turn to yourself and study your own failings. Then you will forget your anger.

~ Epicetus

Anger can be a great teacher. When you get triggered to feel anger, there is a clear place inside of your body that is activated. Another person might not even be bothered by the same situation, but you are. Why is that? That is your job to figure out, so you can heal that place inside of you that gets triggered and is sensitized.

There is a wonderful tool that can help in those cases called "The Work" that was developed by Byron Katie. She says that when a strong emotion like anger is triggered there is a great opportunity to examine it, so the war inside each one of us can end. The tool can be used freely and can be found in the internet under: "Judge your neighbor worksheet". Below is a simplified version of her method.

GOT ANGER?

HEALING PATH:

In the below sentence, substitute A with the name of a person that triggered your anger, and B with the reasons your anger has been triggered.

I am angry at…A…because…B…

(E.g. I am angry with my partner because he/she doesn't listen to me.)

Then ask yourself:
1. Is B true? (E.g. Is it true that he/she doesn't listen to me?) Just answer with yes or no, no explanations whatsoever.
2. Is B absolutely true? (E.g. Is it absolutely true that he/she doesn't listen to me?) Again, just a simple yes or no (usually the answer tends to be no, and we might start having a glimpse of why not (e.g. They might listen to me, in their own way).
3. How do you react/feel when you believe B? (E.g. When you believe that he/she doesn't listen to you.) Most people respond with some negative words such as: tense, frustrated, sad, annoyed, I lash out, I close up, etc.
4. Who would you be without the B thought? Usually the answers are: happier, calmer, more relaxed, etc.

This shows that not all thoughts are true and believable. Choosing which thoughts are helpful versus which ones are hurtful can save the day!

CHAPTER 9

ANGER AND LOVE

Heaven has no rage like love to hatred turned, nor hell a fury, like a woman scorned.

~ William Congreve

Women in general are the ones that create and nurture relationships, and they protect them fiercely. If someone dares to sever that bond, women can become quite unsavory. Much is needed to maintain a healthy relationship, including knowing how love is shared and felt. To assist with that, the psychologist Gary Chapman has developed the five languages of love, which define how people express love. The 5 languages of Chapman are: words of affirmation, quality of time, gifts, acts of service, and physical touch.

Based on the work of Gary Chapman and his 5 love languages, and my own observation in private practice I expanded them to the 12 languages of love. They are based on astrological concepts of the planet of love, Venus, and the 12 signs of the zodiac.

Astrology is a very ancient esoteric science, with a history of more than 3,000 years. Not everyone believes that it has validity, however I have seen firsthand, as this knowledge can broaden self-knowledge and self-consciousness.

People tend to give love in the way they feel loved, and if when languages are different it can create disconnect and disappointment.

HEALING PATH:

Identify you and your loved one's languages below.

118

1. **Acting** – They love being active together, doing sports, creating something new and keep moving.
2. **Sensing** – They enjoy a delicious meal, appreciate natural beauty and scents, listen to music, hug and caress each other.
3. **Communicating** – They love to talk about everything, to meet friends, to travel and are stay connected to the present.
4. **Feeling**– They curl up on the couch, seek strong emotional connection and care for loved ones.
5. **Shining** – They do grandiose things, are strong and proud, protect the weak and enjoy the spotlight.
6. **Working** – They enjoy working together, to become better, they appreciate little things and live in health.
7. **Relating** – They love to be partnered up, are pleasant, gentle and polished, enjoy living with sophistication.
8. **Deepening** – They love to merge their souls, deep and intimately, and commit to an unbreakable bond.
9. **Expanding** – They thrive by opening the horizons, travel far, have visons, and fun; and delight in the vastness of what this world has to offer.
10. **Progressing** – They work on the relationship, slowly, thoroughly and steadily, not taking it for granted and serving higher goals.
11. **Freeing** – Being together, yet independent, open to new possibilities, free of traditions, and old bonds.
12. **Merging** – They flow as one, spread universal love, peace and harmony to the heal the pain of the world.

Did I offer peace today? Did I bring a smile to someone's face? Did I say words of healing? Did I let go of my anger and resentment? Did I forgive? Did I love? These are the real questions. I must trust that the little bit of love that I sow now will bear many fruits, here in this world and the life to come.

~ Henri Nouwen

You can leave your mark, every day, a little bit. Make today better than yesterday. Anger can turn people into Beasts, and then a *Belle* (as in *Beauty and the Beast*) is needed to tame it. How does *Belle* do it? She brings curiosity, empathy, kindness, strength, determination, and patience to the task. Do it like *Belle*, first bring peace, a smile, forgiveness, healing and love to the self; and later all these attitudes can be spread to help others on their path away from "beastly" anger, towards love and peace.

HEALING PATH:

Answer the below questions, which expand on the questions in the quote.

1. Did you offer **peace** today? When? Where? How? To whom? Why? What did you learn from it?

2. Did you bring a **smile** to someone's face today? When? Where? How? To whom? Why? What did you learn from it?

3. Did you say words of **healing and comfort** today? When? Where? How? To whom? Why? What did you learn from it?

4. Did you **let go** of your anger and resentment today? When? Where? How? To whom? Why? What did you learn from it?

5. Did you **forgive** today? When? Where? How? To whom? Why? What did you learn from it?

6. Did you **love** today? When? Where? How? To whom? Why? What did you learn from it?

Red is such an interesting color to correlate with emotion, because it's on both ends of the spectrum. On one end you have happiness, falling in love, infatuation with someone, passion, all that. On the other end, you've got obsession, jealousy, danger, fear, anger and frustration.

~ Taylor Swift

Correlating color with concepts is an antique practice. There is a form of therapy that is centuries old and uses the power of color to cure diseases. It is called chromotherapy. It uses electromagnetic radiation and is based on the premise that light is energy. Each color has a different wavelength, frequency, and quantity of energy. According to chromotherapy, the body is stimulated by colors, and each organ or part has its own vibration that correlates to the vibration of the different colors. In the Hindu tradition, the concept of having energy vortexes in our body that resonate with different color vibrations is called *chakras*.

HEALING PATH:

The color red is the color of fire and blood; it is associated with anger, danger, strength, courage, power, and determination as well as passion, desire, and love. It enhances human metabolism, increases respiration rate, and raises blood pressure. It has very high visibility, which is why stop signs, stoplights, and fire equipment are usually painted red. In marketing red is used to stimulate quick decisions such as 'Buy Now' or 'Click Here'.

If you need to add or increase any of the "red" qualities described above, try a session of chromotherapy. Below is a short list of what each color is used for.

Red stimulates the body and mind and increases circulation.

Yellow stimulates the nerves and purifies the body.

Orange heals the lungs and increases energy levels.

Blue has anti-inflammatory qualities.

Indigo alleviates skin problems.

Green calms the nervous system.

White regenerates.

The ego mind both professes its desire for love and does everything possible to repel it, or if it gets here anyway, to sabotage it. That is why dealing with issues like control, anger, and neediness is the most important work in preparing ourselves for love.

~ Marianne Williamson

The ego thrives on dysfunctional love where there is no understanding or empathy, only fighting to be right, persecuting others, or being in a state of victimhood, waiting to be rescued. Sometimes we are the ones doing the rescuing in an attempt to appear strong and wise, yet all we are doing is deflecting from taking an honest and objective look at ourselves. Stephen Karpman described these states in the "drama triangle": Victim, Persecutor, and Rescuer. Sometimes these roles define and become a part of us.

HEALING PATH:

Are you caught in the drama triangle?

Rescuers – Are helpers, fixers and caretakers. They tend to smother, control and manipulate others to feel better. Their greatest fear is that they will end up alone, so they encourage dependency, to avoid abandonment.

Persecutors – Believe others can't be trusted. They are aggressive to self-protect, they hide their pain and the anger, and they try to change and discipline others. They like to be right! Their greatest fear is powerlessness.

Victims – Believe they cannot take care of themselves, see themselves as damaged, are needy, and show themselves as weak, fragile or not smart enough. Their greatest fear is that they won't make it.

HONESTY IS THE WAY OUT OF THE TRIANGLE.

Healthy Rescuers nurture, empower and encourage self-responsibility. They trust that people know how to get through difficult times.

Healthy Persecutors have a deep-seated sense of justice, believing in the use of power and assertiveness.

Healthy ex-victims learn to assume responsibility for themselves, practice self-care, problem solving and leadership skills.

CHAPTER 10

CREATIVE ANGER

For me, comedy starts as a spew,
a kind of explosion, and then you
sculpt it from there, if at all. It
comes out of a deeper, darker side.
Maybe it comes from anger, because
I'm outraged by cruel absurdities,
the hypocrisy that exists everywhere,
even within yourself, where it's
hardest to see.

~ Robin Williams

There is no denying that Robin Williams had an uncanny creative talent for humor. Most people are not like him, yet learning can be gained from the wisdom of his words. Earlier, a wonderful technique called Neuro-linguistic Programming (NLP) was mentioned, that allows the transfusion of two states (impatience to patience). NLP also offers some strategies on how to turn anger into humor.

HEALING PATH:

1. Start thinking about a situation that triggers anger in you. Could be a onetime event or a recurring one. Visualize it as a movie.

2. Now freeze the one frame in the movie that represents the situation the best, it can be the one that is the most emotionally charged, or any other. For you, which single image in that anger-provoking movie embodies the experience the best?

3. Now bring that one image to mind and look at it in all its colorful details. Try to figure out what exactly brings out the anger in you.

4. Now in your mind, put that picture into a frame, a funny frame, maybe one that has colorful balloons around its edges. Then imagine a funny song as the background music to the scene, carnival music or children's songs for instance.

5. This will create initially a cognitive dissonance, the frame and music does not match the original image, yet the more you stay with it, a new image is formed. That is how comedy is done, and anger can be transmuted into art.

I guess I probably make violent films partly because I can't express my anger in my real life very well.

~ Park Chan-wook

This quote speaks to the concept of defense mechanisms, coined by Sigmund Freud in the 19th century. More specifically, the quote addresses the mechanisms of displacement and sublimation. According to Freud, defense mechanisms are unconscious strategies utilized to protect individuals from the stress, anxiety and overwhelm of having socially unacceptable thoughts or feelings. Defense mechanisms tend to manipulate, deny or distort reality.

Displacement means that anger is being expressed onto a person, an animal, an object or an action that is sometimes less threatening and unrelated to the situation, instead of directing it towards the person who triggered the anger. This ultimately causes more pain and destruction.

Sublimation means that anger is being expressed onto something constructive, and socially accepted, such as making a movie, writing lyrics to a song, boxing, etc., instead of directing it at the person who triggered the anger. This is considered a mature and healthy defense mechanism.

HEALING PATH:

Think back on your own life and list the times you used displacement as a defense mechanism against repressed anger.

By looking at these situations in the past, from your current point of view, what could you have done differently?

Has someone else in your life used displaced anger onto you? Describe the situation, to gain some awareness.

Have you ever seen someone using displacement on someone else? Describe the situation, to gain some awareness.

Think about a creative way that you or that other person could have used to sublimate the anger instead of displacing it.

It's usually a big kind of vent of frustration or anger or sadness that puts me in the right frame of mind to write. It's such a cliché to say that artists write when they're down, but it's true for me. It's a relief to get out what's eating away at my heart or my soul or my head.

~ Ellie Goulding

PUtting your thoughts, emotions, sensations on paper is a great way to find release. Even if you have no intention to publish your writings and you want to keep them private or burn them, there is power in venting on paper. Venting means giving something an outlet. In the case of anger, it means letting it come out verbally in a safe environment. This could be done in person, if you have someone that can be empathic and validate while you vent. If there is no one available, journaling can serve the same purpose. It not only helps release the anger but can actually lead to creative solutions.

HEALING PATH:

There is an art to journaling, it is described in 3 steps.

1. First start writing down anything and everything that is on your mind, no filter, no judgment, just let it rip. Don't even care about grammar or orthography simply let it all out. After the bulk of your anger is out, and you start feeling calmer and less angry, there might be a point in which you have to start to think about what to write. There is this break, this silence... that is a magical moment to reach into deeper levels within you.

2. When you get to the place of pause, keep writing what is inside of you. Record even simple thoughts such as *I feel stupid right now, because I have really nothing else to say, but I read in a book that I should continue writing.* Write down your thoughts, emotions, physical sensations, and keep going. Then you will reach a second point of quietness. When you get to that point, ask yourself:

3. What needs to be expressed through me right now? Where do I need to direct my attention? Or ask another question that matters to you, and then be very quiet inside and simply listen. The messages that come up at this point come from a different place inside of us. They have a different tone, usually quieter, nicer, simpler and wiser.

CHAPTER 11

ANGER
AND
FORGIVENESS

Genuine forgiveness does not deny anger but faces it head-on.

~ Alice Miller

Forgiveness is a strong act that can lessen or even eliminate anger. Forgiveness means overcoming negative feelings towards a transgressor, being willing to not seek vengeance, and letting go of judging the person who hurt us. Forgiveness is done by the person who has been hurt. If the perpetrator is willing to make genuine amends and take responsibility for his/her wrongdoings, that will make the process of forgiveness easier.

HEALING PATH:

Hong and Jacinto (2011) created a therapeutic process to facilitate forgiveness. It is wise to go through the process with a therapist. Here is a summary of the steps:

1. Think about the person/event that you want to forgive. What images come to mind? Pick the 3 strongest ones.
2. Write about these three experiences, and how they connect to the person/situation.
3. Now think of 10 more experiences (positive and/or negative) with the person/situation.
4. When thinking about all the combined experiences, what thoughts come to mind?
5. Of all the experiences, which one stands out the most? Write about it.
6. Write a letter to the person to be forgiven. Do not mail the letter. Discuss the reasons for the anger in the letter.
7. Get two chairs. Sit in one of the chairs and read the letter aloud facing the empty chair, which represents the person that you want to forgive. Once finished reading the letter, move to the other chair and respond to the letter that was just read. Keep the dialogue going, switching chairs, until nothing else is there to be said and there is a will and a sense of being ready to let go and forgive.
8. Draw a future image of when the process of forgiveness is done and long in the past.
9. Think if there is a need for reconciliation. Forgiveness does not require reconciliation. If there is a risk of further harm reconciliation is highly discouraged.

As far as having peace within myself, the one way I can do that is forgiving the people who have done wrong to me. It causes more stress to build up anger. Peace is more productive.

~ Rodney King

Forgiveness is done for oneself. According to Lewis Smedes, a theologian in the 1900s, "to forgive is to set a prisoner free and discover that the prisoner was you." Forgiveness helps overcome psychological problems and it diminishes bitterness, anger, stress, depression, anxiety, and heartache. It reduces negative thoughts and negative emotions. It improves distorted views we might have of others and helps to mend broken relationships, increasing the possibility of reconciliation. It can even potentially prevent the development of post-traumatic stress.

HEALING PATH:

Below are 4 factors that facilitate forgiveness.

1. **Empathy –** Empathy means to listen non-defensively and work towards developing mutual understanding. It means understanding that people are imperfect and fallible, rather than innately bad or cruel.

2. **Humility –** Humility decreases rationalization and blaming. It helps to take responsibility for one's actions and acknowledge the damage that was done. It increases the ability to express sorrow for pain the other has experienced.

3. **Commitment and hope –** These factors focus on the desire to keep the relationship together. Remember past positive memories of closeness and connection. Positive feelings fuel de desire for shared goals and dreams.

4. **Apology –** Apologies should include an honest and authentic acknowledgment of any wrongdoings, a request for forgiveness, a sincere expression of regret, and a desire to do no future harm. Apologizing also means committing to do whatever is necessary to facilitate healing for the other.

Anger ventilated often hurries towards forgiveness; anger concealed often hardens into revenge.

~ Rodney King

Concealed or suppressed anger can harden into many different emotions and states, and one of them is revenge. One form of silent revenge is using passive-aggressive behavior. It is anger that is expressed in an indirect way, such as using the silent treatment, giving cold/dirty looks, or procrastinating on purpose to make the other person angry.

The term "passive-aggressive" was first used by the U.S. military during World War II, when psychiatrists noticed that soldiers would show passive resistance instead of complying with superior commands.

Passive-aggression is a learned behavior often developed in response to overcontrolling parents. Because it is a learned behavior, it can be replaced by healthier behavior. This is done by developing awareness of the anger behind it, as well as learning and applying assertive behaviors.

HEALING PATH:

How to be with someone who is using passive-aggressiveness:

1. Understand they truly might not know how to express anger assertively.
2. Ask for specifics to get a clear 'yes' or 'no'.
3. Mirror back the mixed signals/statements. "What I hear you say is…"
4. Validate their answers and concerns.
5. Ask them to give solutions to problems and to create consequences in the case of non-accomplishment of the solutions.

How to free yourself from passive-aggressiveness:

1. Become aware of your hidden anger and get clear on its origin.
2. Notice when you give a "yes", when you mean "no".
3. Realize your need to defeat, annoy or get back at others by failing.
4. Stop doing "too much" for others.
5. Choose people who do not pressure you, who accept you as you are, and who can handle confrontation, anger, and support you in being assertive.
6. Get over the fear of being disliked and stop doing things to please others.
7. Use assertive communication skills to let a person know how what they do affects you and makes you feel.

CHAPTER 12

ANGER
AND
SPIRITUALITY

I know, to banish anger altogether from one's breast is a difficult task. It cannot be achieved through pure personal effort. It can be done only by God's grace.

~   Mahatma Gandhi

For Gandhi anger lived in the breast. Where does your anger live? Your head? Your tummy? Your heart? Everywhere? Sometimes here and sometimes there?

In this quote Gandhi refers to a specific location inside the body where the anger expresses itself, and he also speaks about the presence and power of a higher being. This presence is there in the midst of anger, even when it can't be seen or acknowledged. It removes the sense of loneliness that sometimes is part of the anger dynamic, and once called upon, this presence can even help us banish the anger.

GOT ANGER?

HEALING PATH:

Where in your body does the anger show its presence?

1. Once you have identified the location inside of you that senses the anger, just allow for it to be there. No words need to be expressed, no actions need to be taken, just acknowledge and sit with the anger. Have some tea and cookies with your anger!

2. Breathe through the location of the anger, imagine a lot of fresh, crisp, clean air entering that location. Sometimes it is easier to do that with your eyes closed.

3. Just observe the anger dynamics inside of you, no need to redirect it or change it, just look at it. Do not throw judgmental thoughts towards it, that will only make it worse.

4. Try validating it, thinking something like this: I understand the anger, it makes sense to me (even if it doesn't make total sense, try to find at least one aspect that you can agree with).

5. Finally connect with a higher power and ask for help and guidance.

Meditation can help us embrace our worries, our fear, our anger; and that is very healing. We let our own natural capacity of healing do the work.

~ Thich Nhat Hanh

Meditation is a powerful tool. It not only helps us embrace our unpleasant feelings, it creates a safe place for them to manifest. Once manifested, observed and accepted with love and empathy, these strong feelings can deliver the messages they carry and open our minds even further.

Meditation provides a sense of deep relaxation and creates peace of mind, even if it is just for a short time. Regular mediation lowers stress, enhances optimism, and increases mental clarity, awareness and compassion.

HEALING PATH:

How to meditate on anger:

1. Start by sitting in a comfortable position and close your eyes or just bring your gaze down, no need to focus on anything specific.

2. Breathe deeply and slowly and start noticing the spaciousness inside.

3. Locate the anger inside your body, briefly.

4. Move away from the anger and notice all the other body parts that are not affected by the anger, that are just doing their regular bodily duties.

5. Find the place inside your body that is peaceful and calm. Focus on that. Even if the mind tries to focus back on the anger by flooding you with thoughts that justify the anger. Simply direct the mind gently back to the place of peace.

6. Find the place inside your body, out of which healing is generated, and expand that energy throughout the body, especially onto the part that holds the anger.

> *Too much self-centered attitude, you see, brings, isolation. Result: loneliness, fear, anger. The extreme self-centered attitude is the source of suffering.*
>
> ~ Dalai Lama

An exaggerated self-centered attitude in adults is certainly unhealthy and leads to suffering. Yet, teenagers and young adults need a good dose of self-centeredness. This will help them find out who they are, which in turn will help them identify their tribe, find their path to fulfillment, expand their talents, and ultimately learn to become selfless and make this a better world.

HEALING PATH:

Here are some strategies to help in that process:

1. First make a list of all the people you admire, living or dead, that you know in person or not.

2. Then list the qualities that they exhibit that results in your admiration for them. Go through the list of qualities and connect each one with your own life. How is it that you exhibit these qualities? This is the start of a list of what you value and what matters to you.

3. Then during a whole week track all the activities you do.

4. Next to each activity, write down how you feel about it and if it is in sync or not with your values (the ones you uncovered in previous steps).

5. Rate the activities from very meaningful and fulfilling (10) to not at all (0).

6. Brainstorm how you can do more of the high score activities and how you can raise the score on the low score ones. Maybe some activities need to be eliminated for good.

Hopefully this book started you on a path to create a life full of meaning, which will greatly diminish the sense of isolation, loneliness, fear and anger!

In closing…

> *"Your anger is a gift!"*
>
> *Zach de la Rocha*

It is a gift that can help you to grow and change.

We simply need to sit with an uncomfortable feeling, such as anger, without acting on it. It does not imply that we have been wronged; it is often a learned response. Sometimes anger just means that we've broken through dysfunction.

What gifts does your anger bring you?

I hope you enjoyed your journey through this book, and that it has helped you understand and work with your anger in healthier ways.

As I continue to follow my mission in creating a world of healthy minds, feel free to share your feedback or comments, dear reader. I would love to hear from you. Email me at **life@lifeaspects.com** or visit my website, **www.lifeaspects.com**.

With all my love,

Eliane
Oberammergau, Germany
December 2018

ABOUT THE AUTHOR

My mission is to help create a world of healthy minds. Teaching healthy anger is a big part of it. There are many avenues to help others develop healthy anger behaviors. I do this through one-on-one counseling sessions with clients who are ready to make changes.

I have a master's degree in Organizational Counseling and a post-master's in clinical counseling from Johns Hopkins University, and a PhD in Behavioral Health from the International University of Graduate Studies. I am a Licensed Professional Counselor, a Certified Employee Assistance Provider (CEAP), a certified Crisis Counselor (CISM) and a Board Certified TeleMental Health Provider (BC-TMH).

I have worked in a variety of settings and with a variety of clients. I have worked in Community Mental Health Centers, group homes, and addiction centers, as both clinician and supervisor as well as a faculty associate at my alma mater workshop, and as a presenter in public and private settings.

Currently I work as a Military Family Life Counselor, offering counseling to active duty service members and their families on bases throughout the US and abroad and as a virtual therapist to international clients. My culturally diverse background gives me the opportunity to provide psychotherapy services in German, Portuguese, English and basic Spanish.

Made in the USA
Coppell, TX
16 December 2021

69104747R00090